"How long are you going to stay in Rome?" —"Three days."—"Then you will know Rome. And you?"—"Three months."—"You will have an idea about Rome. And you, Sir?"—"I am planning to settle here."— "You will never know what Rome is like."

This anecdote can be applied to all cities —including Budapest.

The visitor coming here for three short days can see everything. He only has to go up to one of the lovely look-outs in Buda and there before him lies the town in all its beauty, for the delight of his eyes, heart, and camera. He can see the river, spanned by beautiful bridges, and the emerald-coloured Margaret Island. On the left bank, Pest, he can see the throbbing city, the stately block of the Parliament building, and, on the right bank, Buda, the Royal Palace, the gothic spire of Matthias Church, and the gardens of the residential quarters. If from there he goes over to Pest by car or bus and rides along the tree-lined Népköztársaság útja (Avenue of the People's Republic), he will arrive at one of the most beautiful spots in the city, Hősök tere (Heroes' Square). From the avenue, straight as a bowstring, he will see, from far off, the huge Millenary Monument standing in the centre of the square. The semicircular colonnade with its statues closes the Avenue of the People's Republic just as characteristically as in Paris the Arc de Triomphe closes the Champs-Élysées. Statues, a large square, museums, a pretty little lake with its gay boats and there, behind the bridge spanning the lake, the trees of City Park and a small castle... an unusual feature being that all its gates, ramparts and turrets were built in different styles and are small-scale copies of different old Hungarian castle gates, bastions and church towers. After making an excursion as far as the ruins of Aquincum, the Roman town and military camp, dating from approximately two thousand years ago, he can enjoy fish soup and stuffed cabbage, Tokaj wine and lively gipsy music..., send his picture postcards saying: "I've been here, I've seen it, now I know what Budapest is like..."

I look at these photographs. I was born here, in this city, I know the majority of the places photographed, and closing my eyes, my imagination can take me among the leafy trees and behind the walls of the houses. The pink chestnut blossoms of a spring walk... a bench behind a statue—that is where I prepared for my matriculation... a grim, five-story tenement house—it was in the cellar that I lived through the siege of Budapest. I look at the photographs and my heart sinks. As a child I wanted to be an explorer, I dreamed about the jungle. I wanted to travel to far-away lands, among wild peaks, to unravel mysteries, to make unknown people and silent stones speak, to find the traces of vanished civilizations. I was attracted by the unknown. And now when I have grown up and passed the prime of life I look at the photographs in this album with dismay. Here it lives, breathes and expands around me—and yet still my native town conceals so many secrets and beauties from me.

Budapest is made of contradictions. Its geographical situation, its reconstructed Castle District, its palaces make it beautiful—but the narrow streets crammed with tenement houses built by speculators at the turn of the century also make it ugly. Hills and plain, river and island, tall houses and single-story hovels, rows of crumbling houses waiting to be demolished and thousands of new, modern homes, crowded, rickety trams and a modern underground, which will be extended into a network—all this is Budapest. Just as the ground on which it was built is full of contradictions; here the Buda Hills and the Great Plain meet, at depth lies a Triassic mountain range and over it a permeable sedimentary layer—it is from this layer that for millions of years the city's thermal springs have been welling up. Under the city, the settling earth is in constant movement, bubbling, clashing, struggling, just as on the surface the history of the town has always been full of change and turbulence. Actually Budapest is a very young city. The union of Pest, Buda and Óbuda came into being only a hundred years ago. But there was a human settlement on the site ten thousand years ago—this is borne out by the finds in Remete barlang (Hermit's Cave), on the outskirts of Buda, and there was an important settlement almost three thousand years ago. Pannonians, Eravisci and Romans came in relays, to be followed in their turn by the peoples of the migration period. Hunnish, Alan, Gepid, Jazyg, Gothic and Avar troops moved across the country to make place for the Hungarians who settled and founded a state here. A crossing-place on the Danube, important from the military and commercial points of view, at the foot of mountains and on the edge of a fertile plain—everybody wanted to gain a footing here, no conqueror by-passed it. During its stormy history it was in turns a boundary of Rome, a besieged fortress, a burnt town; Mongols and Turks sacked it, the Emperor of Austria took revenge on it, and in the Second World War all its bridges were blown up, the majority of its buildings demolished or seriously damaged by Nazi destruction and the siege. Each event—construction and destruction, siege and conquest—changed the image of the town.

Budapest can be known only in this way:

by understanding its history, and with curiosity and amazement. Its values, beauties and treasures lie scattered about: it was not planned with compass and ruler as most modern cities are, and if it does have some homogeneous quarters—like the wonderfully reconstructed Castle District or some of the beautiful new housing estates—they are not really characteristic. The real Budapest is a city of surprises: you are walking along the bustling Fő utca (Main Street) and you suddenly come across some Turkish baths roofed with green-rusted copper. Or in the basement of a new block of flats in Óbuda, you find a Roman mosaic floor representing the drunken Hercules and a tiger stalking a bunch of grapes... In Budapest everything has its history: the little underground railway running under the Avenue of the People's Republic was the first underground on the Continent—it was opened in 1896. Close to the airport is the József Attila housing estate, one of the beautiful modern areas in the city, but up to the Second World War the most miserable slums were there, it was the shame of the city with tens of thousands of starving and shivering families. Speaking about the history of the picturesque little streets, fashionable restaurants and winecellars of the Castle District, one should not forget that after the Second World War scarcely one wall stood intact. The remnants of Hitler's igno-

minious troops remained in that district until February 1945, ravaging, shooting and killing. A San Franciscan pronounces "Golden Gate" with a proud flash in his eyes, Harbour Bridge is dear to the inhabitants of Sydney, the French even have a song about the Pont d'Avignon. But has anyone ever heard the people of Budapest talk about their bridges? After the Second World War none of our bridges was standing. The city was lying paralysed, unconscious, torn apart. Hundreds of thousands volunteered to carry stones for the reconstruction. These bridges are life to Budapest. The construction of the first one (1842–49)—Chain Bridge—is connected with the name of one of the greatest figures in the history of Hungary, Count István Széchenyi. In the reconstruction of the bridges the whole nation was involved.

What can this album say to the foreigners who never visited our country? I would like them to become curious, to feel a longing and sympathy—to come and see what there is here. As for those who have already been here, they will certainly turn over these pages with loving recollection. Sometimes they will say: "Yes, that's how I remember Margaret Island." Or: "This wasn't built when I was there." And when coming to the end of the album, they will perhaps think it would be nice to make a return visit. Budapest is a city to which you should return.

BUDAPEST

Corvina

4, 5, 6

11, 12, 13

15, 16

20, 21, 22

23, 24

25, 26, 27

31, 32

33, 34

55, 56